The Professional Referral Solution

Residential Real Estate
Through Business
Professionals,
An Alternative to Cold Calling

Kevin Craig

The Professional Referral Solution

Printed by:
90-Minute Books
302 Martinique Drive
Winter Haven, FL 33884
www.90minutebooks.com

Copyright © 2016, Kevin Craig

Published in the United States of America

160122-00308

ISBN-13: 978-0692650233
ISBN-10: 0692650237

For more information on 90-Minute Books including finding out how you can
publish your own lead generating book, visit www.90minutebooks.com or call
(863) 318-0464

Here's What's Inside...

Introduction

If you've been in real estate for any length of time, you are bombarded on a weekly basis by people trying to sell you their lead generation programs. Everybody has "a better mousetrap" that is "guaranteed to bring you business." Most of these seem too good to be true—and most are. Everyone makes money except for the Realtor. They often smack of get-rich-quick schemes. "Join our program: We're going to send you leads. We're going to send you clients. We've got buyers in your area". We have all had to wrangle our way off of those calls. We get them every single day.

Before we go any further, I want to make sure you understand that *The Professional Referral Solution* is not a get-rich-quick scheme. It is not a way to make money with very little effort. In fact, in some cases it may require more effort than what you're currently putting in. This is not a work-from-home, at-your-leisure, only-10-hours-a-week, you-can-do-this-on-the-side type of deal. It is certainly not a one-size-fits-all either. What I am proposing here is just not for everyone.

In fact, it's actually a somewhat complex system that is definitely outside the box. I'm not aware of any others who are using this type of system in the same way that we have successfully been using it here for several years. is designed for those who I describe as rainmakers, those who are responsible for generating business for their teams. These people need to be highly competent because they will be dealing with other highly competent clients. These clients typically include attorneys, and those who work at law firms. These types of professionals are highly educated, they're sophisticated, and they like to ask high-end questions. Not everybody is able to speak comfortably to a group like that; however, if you are implementing this solution for your team, you'll want to ensure that your team is polished and able to present in front of groups like this.

If you and your team are looking to expand your business and are searching for a systematic approach to generating somewhat automatic and consistent sales—not leads, but listings—then keep reading!

Enjoy the Book!

I hope this book inspires you to look outside the box for your next wave of business and encourages you to consider business professionals as an alternative to cold-calling and chasing leads.

To Your Success!

Kevin Craig

The Professional Referral Solution

Good afternoon. This is Susan Austin. I'm excited to be here with Kevin Craig. Kevin is going to tell us about his thoughts and ideas on how to grow your real estate business outside the traditional real estate box.

Welcome, Kevin.

Thank you, Susan; it's nice to be speaking with you.

I do things a little bit differently within my team, and there's a reason for that. I'm the managing partner for the S4 Group at Keller Williams Realty, Phoenix. We are a team of 10 people who operate within Keller Williams in Tempe, Arizona. However, we have expanded our team into Las Vegas, Nevada; southern California; and the island of Maui.

The growth of our system started as a result of what we believe is a very unique process that was in high demand. Rather than selecting the areas into which we wanted to go, the areas selected us. For instance, we received calls from law firms that found out what we were doing and asked if we might start up such a program in their areas because they had a need for what we were offering.

We also expanded into Tucson. Tucson is about an hour-and-a-half south of Phoenix. It's a completely different market, but we first expanded into Tucson before there was an expansion program within Keller Williams, and we found that we could easily operate in another city using the exact same model. From that point, we decided that we would see who needed us in their area, and that's how we began to expand.

I've been in real estate for about 12 years. I had a career with the United Parcel Service for 27 years. I worked my way into a senior management position there. UPS® gave me a very good understanding of how to manage teams and how to work with people.

UPS is often referred to as a cross between the Mormons and the Marines because it's very precise, very honest, very disciplined, and has high integrity. Everything moves very, very quickly, and everything is run by a system. It's a well-oiled machine.

My background with a company like that fits very well into real estate. I retired from UPS at age 46 and found a career that didn't start off as a career. It started off as something to keep me busy in retirement, but very quickly I found that I could be successful and have fun doing it. Beyond just selling the real estate, I like the relationship part of it, and I like applying things that I've learned in my previous career to be able to help others grow their businesses as well.

When I was with UPS, I became a "fix-it guy." Over my 27 years, I managed several operations and departments, such as Corporate Security, sorting operations, and internal staff operations. I was transferred around the country, and I was promoted several times, with each promotion requiring a move.

I was typically sent to locations that struggled in particular areas and that needed somebody fresh to come in, take a look, and figure out what part of the core process needed to be redesigned. I spent most of my career in Corporate Security training investigators. UPS at the time had over 350,000 employees which is almost a small society. All societies have issues with theft, fraud, illegal shipments, etc. My group identified problem processes and people and we addressed them. I have some great stories.

I've always been an out-of-the-box thinker. I haven't always believed in going along with the status quo. I had a very wise father who was a very well-respected public figure in the state of California for many years. He was absolutely my greatest business mentor.

My father used to tell me all the time, "Not even a turtle gets anywhere until it sticks its neck out at some point," and, "Always ask yourself, 'If I try something new, what's the worst thing that can happen?' and compare it to the best result." I always believed that at some point you have to try things a little bit differently if you expect to get a different result and you should never be afraid to do so.

When I was brought into new UPS locations, districts, or states that had challenges in certain areas, quite often I looked at the situation with fresh eyes and saw how it could be completely dismantled and put back together in a completely different way. Not every time I did that was I successful, but each time it was a learning experience, and in most cases, I was able to find a way to do things that other people hadn't thought of before.

Even today, there are many things that happen within UPS to which I can say, "I implemented that." Some of the things that are very visible to the public today are things in which I was involved and that helped create a different way of doing business.

Most improvements are made through people and processes. If you peel back the layers of the onion and look to see where things can change, it's going to be in one of those two areas. Real estate isn't any different. It's either the people or the process that can attain and improve a real estate business, and that's what really needs to be evaluated each time you try to see how you can make things better.

I started in real estate at the top of the market. I entered in 2004 in Arizona, when many people were buying homes as fast as they came on the market or even sometimes sight-unseen. People moving in from California couldn't buy houses fast enough. A lot of them called ahead, put offers on properties, and then came out during inspection periods to see if they wanted to stay in the deals. There was a panic that there just weren't going to be enough homes to go around, and that's partly what drove our values sky high.

Of course, what goes up must eventually come down, and, as everybody knows, we had one of the biggest real estate crashes of anywhere in the country. I think Arizona, Florida, and Nevada (specifically Las Vegas), in that order, had the furthest to fall because they had climbed the highest.

The situation was almost like a utopia when I first entered, and then I saw things at about the worst they'd ever been. People walked away from houses, foreclosures increased, and people quit buying because the values were dropping so fast. For a while it was pretty scary, with everyone wondering how anybody was ever going to sell another house. Panic set in for many people and many Realtors went back to corporate jobs if they could find them.

That's the kind of market I came into, but I'm one of the survivors. I not only made it through that period, but I was also able to grow a very successful real estate business and team during that time. We've done so well that now we've been inducted into Gary Keller's Top 100. Keller Williams is the largest real estate brokerage in North America and one of the largest in the world. We have over 100,000 agents, and we're in Gary's Top 100, which puts us in the top 1%. That position means I and my group get invited to a lot of things, which includes Masterminds with Gary Keller, which is an opportunity to share some of what we're doing with Gary and his staff. It gives us exposure to a lot of the parts of the business that we wouldn't have been exposed to otherwise, all a result of hard, the volume of business that we've done and the reputation we've developed.

In 2014, we closed a little over $33 million in gross sales. In 2015, we ended with $47 million. Our goal for this year, 2016, is to hit $65 million, and our plan to do that does not have anything to do with adding people, which may come as a shock to you. Many people believe that in order to grow your business, you have to continue to add people and grow your team, and that's not necessarily true. While most teams do grow, again, our approach is outside the box.

Many people use the same system of adding people in order to add more business. That's just not what we do. We're called the S4 Group (Sales, Service, Synergy, and Significance), and we're becoming fairly well-known throughout the Phoenix metro area as well as the other markets in which we work. I see our team as a brokerage within a brokerage. Everything that is transacted within my team does not go under my name. If a listing is brought in by one of my agents, my agent lists that property under the S4 Group and their own name. If an agent sells a property, the purchase contract goes under that particular agent's name. As the owner, I just get a small cut of the commission— just like a brokerage. You would have to look at each of the eight licensed agents I have on my team to be able to track our total volume.

Many people research transactions in my name in order to see the S4 production but it doesn't work like that. Personally, I do more business than the average agent. I typically do about $10 to $12 million in a year. The $47 million and soon to be $65 million, however, comes from the combined efforts of all of my agents. I keep everything under their names. They participate in team agreements and team splits, and by using our system's programs and team structure, I still benefit from each thing they do. Meanwhile, they get to have their own identities within my team and not feel that everything is being worked under Kevin Craig and that Kevin Craig is going to get all the recognition.

I have several friends who have had large teams, and it's very common for me to hear things like, "We used to have a really large team, but a large team brings along large headaches," and, "We used to have a big team, but we decided to scale back and go back to just a couple of us because it was a lot easier to manage."

I've found, I think, a perfect number of people. We have eight active agents, including me, who are actively buying and selling. I'm still in production to a small extent, but not as much as I was at one time. We have a couple of support staff as well. One is a licensed agent and does all of our transaction coordination, and the other is an internal sales associate who is not licensed. She's not licensed because we want her to be able to speak to people not as though she's trying to sell them something but more as a customer-care individual, who helps people.

How the Professional Referral Solution Started

Right after I got into the real estate market and started my own, individual business, the bottom fell out of the real estate market here in Arizona, and we started to see the REOs (real-estate owned properties), owned by the banks, pop up. People started walking away from their homes in droves, which caused a lot of panic within the real estate market in some areas.

Other areas thought they were immune to what was going on because they had more expensive and more prestigious housing. That wasn't the case. Short sales came on the scene. Banks were willing to sell properties for less than what was owed, but there had to be a negotiation with the bank to do so. This was all new.

I know that short sales have existed for years, but they had been rare and the level at which they were happening within Phoenix was new to most of the agents in the real estate market. Many said they didn't want to participate in the short sales. They would rather wait until the market came back and continue doing equity sales." Everybody thought the market was going to come back very quickly, but some of the economists were telling us otherwise. They said we could be in it for the long-haul. It took almost ten years for us to start making a turn and bring our real estate market back.

I wasn't excited about doing the short sales, but I was very intrigued by them because, once again, they were outside the box. They weren't something that everybody else was doing, and they were complicated. They weren't something that everybody learned about in real estate school or that was taught in most brokerages at the time.

In the early stages, if you wanted to learn about short sales, it was trial by fire. You had to jump in and learn how to do it yourself. It seemed complicated, but I wanted to get involved. I found a couple of attorneys from a real estate law firm who were teaching a seminar about short sales. I think their primary objective was to scare us agents out of doing short sales so they could capitalize on some of that business and negotiate the short sales themselves.

As I listened to the presentation, I started to think that there wasn't anything they were doing that I couldn't figure out how to do myself. I could probably learn this if I got a little bit of help.

I retained one of the attorneys who gave the seminar, which turned out to be one of the best investments I ever made. It's still a great friendship that goes on today. He helped turn my whole real estate business around. I had him help me put together a short-sale process that worked legally and also worked according to the department of real estate. At that time, there were no disclosures or addendums for short sales. I think a lot of brokers and even agents were worried that, some day, anybody who participated in a short sale from a real estate standpoint would ultimately be sued. Some thought we'd be seeing commercials on TV that said, "If you participated in a short sale, call 1-800-THE-EAGLE, and we'll help you sue your real estate agent." A lot of people wanted to stay away from that possibility.

However, I thought that if I had an attorney to help me do it, there'd be less of a chance that I would be left open for a lawsuit. This attorney and I put together disclosures and then ran those disclosures—and the addendums we created—by my broker.

The broker, who was extremely experienced, looked at those documents and decided whether or not they fit within the real estate world.

Therefore, between the legal world and the real estate world, we perfected a short-sale process that we thought was pretty ironclad. Next I had to find people willing to help me do short sales. There were a few agents that had the aptitude to do them, who I brought on to work with me because I felt that there was more business than I would be able to handle myself. We became quite successful.

Some of the early pioneers in short sales were teaching seminars, and we were just quietly working behind the scenes, not looking for notoriety, doing our own short sales.

We became so versed in them that many other brokerages gave us referrals for their clients because, again, they had the attitude of not really wanting to get involved in the process. It was too messy for them, but since we knew how to do it, they sent their clients to us, and we gave them referrals. In that way, they could still do the short sales without actually getting their hands dirty.

That led us to work in short sales for a few other brokerages and quite a few other agents around the valley. We found a couple of short-sale negotiators that were really well-versed in dealing with the banks. We found one that was originally hired as one of the first short-sale negotiators for Bank of America. She became one of their trainers and trained most of their internal negotiators in how to work short sales. Eventually, we more or less hired her away to be our short-sale negotiator, and that was certainly a leg up that we had on some of the others trying to get into the short-sale business.

Another thing we learned was that there were other areas which had been affected by the short sales, such as the bankruptcy court system. We found that, at one point when the bankruptcy court had properties that had equity, the bankruptcy trustee took control of the properties. They would force sales, and the proceeds from those sales were used towards the bankruptcy file. That means that some of the money in the proceeds went to satisfy some of the unsecured creditors, such as credit card companies. Some of the proceeds were actually used to compensate the attorneys and the bankruptcy trustee that performed the bankruptcy.

In a bankruptcy, a trustee sits down with a homeowner and holds a special hearing to determine what the homeowner gets to keep; what they needed to sell; and what the rules will be moving forward in order to get all of their debt cleared, so that they can get a fresh start.

When the housing market crashed, there was no longer equity in the properties, everything changed for the bankruptcy court. Suddenly they were no longer able to use equity from properties and apply it towards their cases—there wasn't any. It made things more difficult. The court ended up handing the properties back to the banks in essence saying, "There's no equity. Here, Mr. Bank, you can have it."

The property would go back to the bank as an REO, and the bank would sell it as an REO. We found that if we could solve a problem for the bankruptcy trustees and get some funds from the bank to be able to cover some of the unsecured debts; it would actually help the banks not have to deal with a higher inventory of properties. It also helped the trustees because they were able to apply some of the funds we got from the bank towards the unsecured creditors. It helped homeowners because they were able to get out from underneath their mortgages, receive relocation funds and keep foreclosures off their credit reports.

We came up with a pretty good system that worked well, but the frontline people at the banks couldn't get their heads around it. The banks could not understand what the role of the trustee was. To make it more complicated, every time we called the bank, it seemed we talked to somebody new, even employees who hadn't even been doing short-sale negotiation the week before. Maybe they were working in a completely different industry and had only been brought into the bank because of the tremendous increase in short sale volume.

We did a whole lot of banging our heads against the wall, trying to get the banks to understand what we were doing. In the process, we learned that what we'd been doing all along was establishing relationships with many law firms that represented the debtors or people who owned the homes that were in bankruptcy. We decided to utilize those relationships.

We explained to the law firms what we were able to do and how we could benefit their clients through negotiating short sales versus having the trustees just hand properties back to the bank. When we did that, our business took off because we were able to present a solution to a problem that they had within the bankruptcy court system as a whole. Because we had worked with the judges, because we had worked with the trustees, and because we were now working with the attorneys, we had a pretty good reputation for being able to get short sales done. We found ways that our process could benefit homeowners a lot more than just allowing keeping their houses from going through a foreclosure. Our process benefited the attorneys because they were able to provide an alternative solution to their clients which made them look good, and it also solved a problem for the courts and the trustee. It made a messy situation a lot less messy.

We grew our business to the point that we had relationships with more than 35 law firms here and in the other markets we were working in. We've continued to grow these relationships over the years.

Then a question arose: Do we continue to grow our business outside of our market area here, or do we teach others our process so they can benefit? We decided to do a little bit of both.

There are some markets in which we'd like to keep working, and there are some markets in which I'm perfectly fine coaching others, so they can jump in and do this type of unique business. Again, it's not a one-size-fits-all process. It's not necessarily going to work for everybody and their types of businesses. It is just one more tool that a team could use to generate listing opportunities for their team or for an individual who is growing a team.

13

With this book, I want to explain what we're doing, where we're doing it, why we're doing it, and when we're doing it. The exact how will come later because, at some point, I'll need to be able to provide much more detailed information in the form of specific scripts, specific documents, and specific processes that we've learned over time. I'm planning to hold seminars to cover these areas as this goes to print. We want to make sure that everybody is doing this the right way and that we can systemize it. This is a conceptual book in that some people may read it and say, "No, this is not for me."

Others may read it and say, "This is exactly what I'm looking for. I think I want to take this to the next level." I wrote this book because I decided I want to teach what I've learned. I like speaking to groups and sharing some of what I've learned over the years. Whether it's a group of attorneys, a group of trustees, or a group of agents, I have no problem explaining more about what I've learned. I definitely don't talk over everybody's head—my vocabulary isn't large enough. I think I talk on the same level that I understand things, which is probably more of a third or fourth grade level. I think I could do a good job of presenting this in layman's terms, but also teach people how to be able to speak to attorneys within their language and at their level.

Outside the Box

This is not rocket science; it's just a way of connecting all the dots of what would seem to be a very complex process. The good news is that it's not, if you follow the right systems and procedures. There's no reason that anybody has to go through the five and six years of inventing the wheel that we already have.

The reason that this may seem new is because it goes against the typical way in which teams generate volume and grow themselves. Many teams use a system that is based on calling expired, cancelled, and for-sale-by-owner people from lists. There are big call centers that mega-agents have put together to do nothing but make these cold calls, or their agents are required to work three or four hours every morning, making cold calls and seeing if they can get appointments. It's a proven system that absolutely works. People have grown huge real estate businesses by doing it, but, once again, it's not one-size-fits-all. Not everybody can do that. People have told me, "I just don't think I'm going to be a success in real estate because I can't sit down and make cold calls for four hours every morning."

There are ways of doing real estate that don't involve cold-calling, but most of those methods are not taught. What is taught are systems based on huge numbers of cold calls, systems that provide the phone numbers, systems that do the dialing, and systems that provide the scripts. Then they teach how to talk to people who have had their current listing expire or has been cancelled, or homeowners who are trying to sell their home themselves as a for-sale-by-owner, all in hopes of setting an appointment so they or someone else on their team can visit with them again in person.

The reason I don't do that is because I'm not the type of person who enjoys making those types of calls. I also have people working on my team of 10 who are not cut out for that either. We don't want to make cold calls. We also don't want to go through the hassle of creating or finding additional office space to be able to house a call center or go through the headache of purchasing phone systems and headsets. A lot of the groups that use this technique have a significant amount of turnover, so they also need to have people who do almost full-time hiring and training.

Within our brokerage, there's a great system for interviewing and hiring people, which I frankly haven't had the need to utilize because I don't hire; I select. I have plenty of people that want to work on my team because they see how we operate, and I choose people who I think will be good fits in the event that somebody leaves my team.

That does happen. For instance, I had somebody who passed the state bar exam after several years of law school and wanted to become an attorney, so they left real estate to start up their own law firm. One of my agents decided to move back to the East Coast to be near grandchildren. I can't fault people for doing that, and we do replace them, but we're not hiring constantly because people are leaving saying, "I just can't handle this type of work." For the most part, the people who work with me end up staying. One agent has been with me for 12 years.

The Numbers That Are
and Aren't Tracked

Within call centers, the goal is to set appointments, but an appointment doesn't necessarily result in a listing or a sale; it's just an appointment. In many cases, teams making cold calls are competing with other cold call because there are so many different groups calling the same lists of people with expired listings, canceled listings, and for-sale-by-owners. Often, there may be four or five people interviewing for the same listing.

For this method to work, there also has to be a pretty amazing listing presentation, and this gets extremely competitive also. There are companies that sell systems to help produce listing presentations. Cold call groups track conversion rates to see how many calls a team has to make in order to generate a certain number of listing appointments and how many listing appointments they have to make in order to generate actual face-to-face meetings because people end up cancelling appointments as well. Then they have to figure out how many people they need to sit down with, face-to-face, before they get an actual listing.

I think if you were to calculate the true cost of securing a listing with this method, it would be pretty substantial because there's a lot of background work that goes into getting each one of them.

We're always looking at the number of units that are sold, as well as the gross sales. Nobody else seems to look at gross sales per agent, but it's a very telling number.

When I spent my time working in for UPS, it was very common for various inside operations to compete in productivity in the same way that agents compete for sales, units, those kinds of things. But it's very hard to do an apples-to-apples comparison when some operations are large, and some operations are small. Some operations process thousands and thousands of packages while others process a smaller number. Some operations have hundreds of people, and some have just a few.

UPS tracks how many packages per man-hour are processed. If you divide the total number of packages into the total number of hours it takes to process those packages, you have an apples-to-apples comparison. Industrial engineers would calculate what a fully efficient operation is capable of producing at its full potential. If an operation is capable of producing 200 packages per man-hour, and it actually hit 200 packages per man-hour, it would be deemed to be running at 100% effective. If it was running at say 190 packages per man-hour, then it's 95% effective. In that way, you can do an apples-to-apples comparison between operations.

For some reason we don't do that in real estate. Instead, we look at the gross sales, we look at what the total number of sold units are, but we don't track how many total agents and staff it requires to produce those types of numbers. I know there are groups with call centers that have 30 to 40 people making phone calls to try to close $50–$60 million in sales each year. I'm able to do that same volume with about eight agents and two administrative people, so my sales per agent is much higher, which means that my agents make more money individually, which also means I have higher morale and a higher job satisfaction rate. My people don't leave.

That's another reason why I don't have to recruit non-stop. I select because other agents see what everybody on my team is making. It's not a big secret in a brokerage like ours where all the numbers are pretty much public. They can all see that the majority of the agents on my team are also the top producing agents in the whole office. It's no accident that all of these top producers have come together on one particular team. That's just a huge benefit. We can look at our percentage of effectiveness and make sure that we're producing a high amount of results with a small number of people. That creates a lot of friendly competition within our own team and generates even more sales for everyone.

Agent Turnover

Agent turnover is one thing that I don't have to worry about much, while many teams spend most of their time worrying about it. They have to decide who they can recruit, while I decide who I want to select. If you're an agent who sells less than one house per month, or your team has agents selling less than one house per month, you have to do a lot of recruiting. When you're a team like mine, with agents that are selling four or more homes per month, you get to do a lot of selecting because there are many people who will want to be a part of what it is you're doing.

Another benefit to the program that we've developed and the system that we have is the way we go about generating our business. Again, we think outside the box. Many groups farm areas. They knock on 25 doors, hoping to get one lead or one person who will talk to them. We knock on one door and see if they have 25 people who they would be willing to refer to us.

You could spend an entire week knocking on doors to find someone who wants to sell their house, or you could systematically target business professionals that are doing the type of business that fits right within your wheelhouse. If you have the right approach, you have the right scripts, and you have the right things to present to them and show them that you can service their clients; you can knock on the door of one business and have them refer 20 or 25 of their clients to you.

That's essentially what we have done when I say that we work with over 35 law firms here in the Phoenix metro area. Those 35 law firms all give us multiple referrals because they understand that we can solve a problem for them and their clients.

We use essentially the same type of script that's used by the agents knocking on doors and farming. As long as you don't mind talking to attorneys, talking to receptionists, and talking to office managers, it's not very different than talking to homeowners at their front doors.

It's very difficult to walk into an attorney's office without an appointment and meet face to face with that attorney. Fortunately, we have a process for that, which makes it more of a warm introduction than a cold call. We also don't have to deal with people hanging up or slamming doors in our faces.

The worst-case scenario is that we set up an appointment to find out that somebody got called into court and can't meet with us. Then we reschedule. We do a lot of our attorney meetings over lunch. It's very pleasant to have a meeting over lunch, but it's very difficult to try to set up meetings over lunch when you're cold calling or farming a neighborhood.

The Advantage of Working with Professionals

Another benefit of our business is that we actually work with professionals.

Ninety-five percent of the referrals we get turn into listings. We're not trying to set an appointment to get in front of them to see if we can get their business. Once we've completed the appointment, they understand what we do, and they've got all of our systems clearly in their heads, they call us, and it's not to give a listing presentation; it's to fill out listing paperwork. Ninety-five percent of the time we're filling out listing paperwork on the first client visit.

The reason I say 95% and not 100% is that there are some cases where we sit down with the client and the best thing for them is not to sell their house. We try to do the right thing for them. I believe it's also impressive to the law firms to see that it's not a matter of us trying to fulfill our needs and wants, but to fill their clients' needs and wants. On occasion it actually helps us to be able to properly advise somebody that selling their house is not what's in their best interest. This isn't really about getting referrals, but getting leads that actually give us business.

If you follow our model and our system, the benefit is that you're able to receive actual leads from your transactions with law firms. They refer their own clients; these are people with whom they have relationships. I think we all know that some of the people that individuals trust the most are their attorneys. When a person's attorney advises them that I'm the right person to call or that my team is, that gives us a great deal of credibility that we just can't get by knocking on doors in a farming area.

How to Find Business Professionals to Work With

The Professional Referral Solution means no auditions and no listing presentations; however, we do sit down and explain how we operate and how the system works. We have a process through which we take them to determine what the right thing is for them and explain next steps, but we don't have to worry about having the latest and greatest laser show presentation with 3D imagery and drone flyovers because that's really not what they want to know about. They want to know how we can help them in their current situation.

We're also not competing. There are no other agents that we have to worry about getting there before we do unless there's a fluke situation. The firms that we work with do not send multiple agents. They send one whom they trust, who they know will treat their clients right, and who they know has the right systems and the best reputation. That's why we get that kind of business.

This isn't necessarily limited to law firms. This could be applied to just about any industry if you follow the same type of system. I've considered writing a second book that discusses some of the other industries that we're currently going into. We're taking the exact same model, the exact same system, the exact same processes, and almost the exact same scripts and applying them to a completely different industry, outside of law, that still benefits people and provides them with opportunities to get out of tough situations. Our process can be applied to virtually any industry, and we're already working on that in other parts of Arizona.

Why Law Firms Are a Great Fit for the Professional Referral Solution

I want to explain how you go about identifying the right law firms. First, you have to select the right field of law. Just like in the medical profession, all attorneys don't service all types of law; they may even have some specialty areas.

Everybody wants to deal with divorce. It seems like when I talk to agents who want to work with attorneys, they all mentioned divorce first because somehow they believe that they all generate multiple transactions: You sell the client's home, and you buy a house for the husband, and then you buy a house for the wife. That sounds good in theory, but it doesn't always work out that way. There are a lot of things you need to do to be able to work with divorce situations. We sometimes talk to people about how to become special commissioners to the court because in many cases you have to be court-appointed, especially if you're dealing with a husband and a wife that can't agree on a real estate professional to use. There's a way to take care of that very easily, and we know the process.

The real estate process becomes more complicated with divorce. In some cases, you have to meet with two different people about the same thing, two different times, and you're doing twice the amount of work. You meet with the husband, then you meet with the wife; you get documents signed by the husband, and then you get documents signed by the wife. Any time there's follow up, you meet with both parties. Divorce, therefore, is certainly one avenue, but it's not the only avenue, and I would suggest that it's not always the best avenue.

The Upside to Bankruptcy

Bankruptcy, on the other hand, has huge benefits. First, people in bankruptcy often have a real need to sell, for the most part, especially if the court has ordered that they liquidate their houses to take care of unsecured creditors or because their houses are major source of their debt.

When a house has a lot of equity, a person tries to hang onto it in bankruptcy, but when a house is a major part of their debt, they get rid of it. If you have the right type of short-sale system, then this may fall right in your wheelhouse. For the most part, the clients are very cooperative because there's an end goal that benefits both the husband and the wife together. They're not on opposite sides on this but rather trying to do it together.

You do need to know some basic bankruptcy law, such as the order that things happen and what various processes are called; however, it's not anything that you couldn't learn on the Internet. You could Google "bankruptcy" and learn quite a bit about it.

You don't have to be a bankruptcy attorney to do bankruptcy real estate. You just have to understand some of the terminology and some of the unique areas that real estate and bankruptcy have in common. That's another thing we'll be teaching in seminars. Remember, you're doing the real estate transaction; you're not doing the legal work. You have to be able to understand what's happening, but you don't have to be legally qualified to actually do it.

Why Elder Law Is a Growing Source of Referrals

Another of the other areas that we're exploring as a solid professional referral source is elder law. Elder law is fairly new; not many people have heard about it or are familiar with it. Elder law is a very specialized field of law that protects the elderly, who are often taken advantage of in our society. They're not just taken advantage of by scammers on the Internet; sometimes they're taken advantage of by sales people, including real estate agents. Lawyers who practice elder law are constantly looking for reputable real estate agents with whom they can work and who can help and be advocates for their seniors.

However, you have to understand how seniors operate. Seniors operate on a little bit of a different level than other generations because they really prefer things to be simple. You have to be able to provide very simple solutions to whatever problems they have. Working with the senior demographic right now is also like standing in front of a tidal wave. We have got so much of that coming because of the demographics that we're dealing with, including the Baby Boomers. Right now, many corporations are putting money into assisted-living centers or assisted-living communities. There's also the opportunity to work with group homes, which are regular homes that have been converted into group facilities to house seniors in home-living situations rather than resort-living situation. These corporations have obviously done their homework; they know what's coming. They know there's going to be a huge need for those things. There's also an opportunity to take our system and convert it to be helping seniors rather than work exclusively with attorneys.

Where to Start Your Professional Referral Solution

Where do you start with this? That's something we can help with. You have to be able to identify the firms and the attorneys that are actually filing the bankruptcies, and we have tools to identify those. I can tell you which firms are filing the bankruptcies and even which attorney is filing within the firm. I can tell you how many they file per month, per quarter, and per year. My team can do a full analysis, and I have access to this for the entire country, to be able to see where you can get the most bang for your buck.

We've also learned that sometimes the big firms aren't necessarily the best firms to deal with; there are positives and negatives in working with firms that file massive amounts of BKs. Sometimes the really large firms that seem to be cranking through the bankruptcies are also the discount firms, and discount firms tend to attract discount clients, which own discount homes. That means you're not going to be dealing with luxury properties. Instead, you're dealing with much smaller homes and, in some cases, mobile homes. Therefore, it's good to know exactly what type of clients the law firms are actually servicing.

We have tools that help with all of those things. We have access to a program that law firms use to exchange information on files, so they can look at past precedents and past fillings. It has all of the information about the client, the property, the case, and the assets. We use this quite a bit, and we try to use a rifle approach instead of the shotgun approach. We don't race out there to try to find every single firm that we can possibly get into. Instead, we have a very, very specific list of criteria for the firms that we want to identify and work with. We have a customized approach for each one of those, with not only scripts, but also the presentations we give when we get in. Again, we want to establish a relationship with them, not see if we can get a quick listing just so we can put a sign in one front yard.

The Importance of Knowing Your Audience

We encourage you to really know your audience. Research the firm, and find out what type of business they do. Many firms have lawyers that specialize in many different fields within those firms. You may get in to speak to one attorney and then find out that there are actually three others within the same firm with whom you should have been meeting, or you may find out that there's a firm that specializes in divorce, but they have one attorney within that firm that handles all the bankruptcies, or vice versa. You may find out that an attorney who practices putting together wills and trusts is also the perfect one to work with senior living, or also has some experience in bankruptcy.

Also research the attorney specifically. Where did they go to law school? What type of law did they practice? Some websites even explain a bit about what their personal interests are in the form of small bios. By going through that process, you can learn more about your audience and set up stepping-stone relationships, so you can understand how to get out-of-state referrals from those lawyers.

We do get referrals for properties that are being sold in other states across the country. For example, if a person is filing a bankruptcy here, it may turn out that they also own a cabin in Montana and a beach home in Florida. This gives us a lot of referral situations. We try to do everything on a formal, yet informal basis, meaning we want to give formal presentations and set up formal relationships, but often attorneys would rather do that over lunch or coffees than sit down in their offices. You can usually get more time with them when they're not sitting at their own desks, and we can teach you how to do that.

Getting Past the Gatekeeper

Getting past the gatekeeper at law firms is often the most difficult thing. Who is the gatekeeper? At most firms it's the receptionist. Receptionists are well-trained to keep people away from the attorneys until they've set up appointments. Even then, they screen them very closely to find out what their needs are before they schedule any appointments.

We've had a lot of success getting past the gatekeepers because we know that, with certain scripts, we're going to be able to get in to meet with attorneys. Doing that may depend on finding out who actually runs the office. Sometimes there's an office manager, and sometimes it's a managing attorney or a managing partner who runs the office. Sometimes those are the real decision-makers, not necessarily the attorney that you plan to sit down and talk to.

You have to evaluate whether you're going to talk to the attorney that actually practices the field of law in which you're interested, or you're going to talk with the person who actually manages the office. I advise you to work with the person who manages the office because they're usually the one who is the real decision-maker; the rest are similar to agents. They work on one task at a time and aren't necessarily looking at the big picture.

Meeting in person is always better than a phone call. If you make a phone call, you're going to get a few seconds. If you can meet with somebody in person, you're going to get a few minutes, and it only takes a few minutes with our system to be able to explain what the benefits are and why that firm might want to have further discussions with you.

The Critical Role That Collateral Plays

Another thing to consider is collateral. What do you bring into a law firm? What will you provide them? A mistake that many people make is providing collateral that they think a law firm is going to want, rather than providing the collateral that the law firm actually wants.

When we started, we had a very comprehensive binder that we provided that had a table of contents referenced by each tab number. It contained every document that we would be using, everything that an attorney would ever want to know about our process. Probably 99%, maybe 100%, of those attorneys put that binder on a shelf and still called us to ask questions because they just didn't want to have to look through a book.

From that, we learned that a one-page document or even a bi-fold document that explains everything that we do and how our system works is really what they're looking for. It's something that they can pass on to a client. We have examples of that kind of document. Again, it took us more than five years to be able to nail down exactly what the correct collateral is, so we would rather share that with you than have you reinvent the wheel.

Face to Face

Face-to-face interviews are absolutely critical. I learned through a university study that when someone walks into a room, the average individual passes some type of a judgment on them as to whether or not they're interested in knowing anything more about that person. That judgment typically takes about six seconds, and in some cases it's less.

When you walk in to present yourself at a law firm, you have to understand that you have about six seconds for that attorney on the other side of the table to determine whether or not they're interested in hearing what you have to say and whether they're interested in setting up a relationship or doing business with you.

How can you be the most presentable, and how can you say the right thing within the first six seconds? You also need to have an elevator pitch. If you have time between floors on an elevator to explain to someone what you do, what would you say? You have to be prepared to present your elevator pitch at all times because, in some cases, that's about how much time an attorney will give you before they determine if they're going to politely ask you to leave their office or if this could be a lifelong relationship.

We can help you with the elevator pitch. We can help you with the right scripting, and we can help you add credibility by explaining how to present things properly. You want to show them that you're a problem-solver and that you can add value to their practice by servicing their clients. You shouldn't walk in and talk about you, all of your background and all of the homes that you've sold. You want to talk about what you can do for them and be a person that solves a problem.

I hate the phrase, "Fake it till you make it," because the professionals can see right through the "faking" and see that you haven't made it. I do encourage people to talk about what they know. Again, you don't have to know everything there is about bankruptcy. You may know just a little bit based on research you've done yourself. Talk about that. Talk about a situation that fits in with the conversation that you're having. Don't fake something because you could end up having your integrity questioned, or your credibility could be shot if the attorney fires questions back, and it turns out that you don't know anything about what you're talking about. Only talk about what you actually know; don't fake it till you make it.

Follow-Ups

I used to have an old boss who would tell me, "Once you sell the car, don't keep talking enough to where you buy it back." Once you've had a conversation with the attorneys and they've agreed to buy in, you need to be done. Any follow-up can be taken care of at a later date, with a subsequent conversation.

There are ways to accomplish follow-ups so that you don't talk yourself right out of a relationship. We have lots of follow-up ideas that we've utilized over the years. We've done pop-bys, we've done lunch-and-learns, and we've done personal notes. We've invited them to speak at events. No one loves speaking about their field like attorneys do. They love speaking about what they've been educated for.

We've joined legal associations. We've worked at state bar association conferences. I've even gone as far as teaching continuing education classes to one of the state bar associations because they're always looking for content and speakers. If I talk about something I know about, as long as I'm not pitching my product or giving an infomercial, I can come in and speak to them. Then, at the end of the seminar, they're certainly welcome to come up and ask me specific questions, take my collateral, take my business card, and call me later. I've received quite a bit of business that way.

Finding a Legal Mentor

If you're going to work on bankruptcies with some of these firms, it's critical that you have somebody on your team or a resource that understands short sales extremely well. Many people, for right or wrong, have used their homes as ATMs and they're completely upside-down when it comes to their properties, so most of the time, you're going to deal with the short-sale situation. Even if the rest of the area seems to be back in equity, the bankruptcy properties are typically upside-down.

There's also a lot of debt that can be incurred after the bankruptcy has been closed. It's called post-petition. Things like HOA fees and taxes continue. The property is still subject to city abatement fines if there are weeds in the yard, etc. Those are still expenses that a client could incur long after the bankruptcy.

They just need to get out of the house to stop some of the bleeding. Many large teams work with investors. Many rainmakers are trying to figure out how to keep their investor pool fed. This is certainly a great opportunity because you have first shot at properties that become available before they actually hit MLS. As long as you're following the rules with the banks and doing everything above-board—disclosing everything and being ethical— you do have an opportunity for your investors to buy some of those properties.

Short Sales

With short sales, it's not always the highest dollar amount that ends up getting the deal. It's the highest and best offer. Often, a cash investor who is willing to take the property "as-is" is the highest and best offer and can end up getting that property and flipping it, which means that you could end up with three sides of the transaction: You sell the property for the original homeowner; you purchase it for the investor—the buy and the sale—and then once the investor remodels it and flips it, you sell it again.

There's just too much competition on MLS these days for investment properties. By the time you see something on MLS; it's pretty much picked clean. This is a way to be able to take a look at the property before anybody else does. Since you're dealing with short sales, many times your investor or your client has several months to research the property, come up with a plan, and work their numbers before they have to put any money into the deal. It's very good to be able to work these kinds of deals with investors.

How to Grow Your Professional Referral Network

If this outside-the-box approach interests you, you can always reinvent the wheel through trial and error and put together the scripts, systems, and processes that we've perfected over the last five years, or you can contact me, and I'd be happy to set up some time with you to talk about systems that I would be more than happy to include. We're putting together information right now that includes ways to be able to get the research into the law firms and attorneys who are doing the cases. We already have the scripts. We already have the logs. We already have the collateral. We already have the process laid out. We even have the emails that we send to everybody to keep them informed and the timeline on which those emails go out to each party to keep them up to speed. Again, communication within real estate is such a critical piece of what we do. It's important to understand that if you jump the gun on this and blow an appointment with a law firm because you don't have all the pieces together, it's probably the only shot you're going to get.

You don't want people jumping in the pool who don't yet know how to swim. You want to make sure that you have everything at your fingertips that you understand it, and that maybe you've been through a course or seminar to understand because it can be a great business down the road if it's done properly.

We'd be happy to provide more information on that when the time comes and make it, more or less, a completely turnkey system that can generate business for anybody's team, whether they're still cold-calling or they want this to be the primary source of their business.

If this sounds good, you can reach us by email at **S4Info@gmail.com**, or call us at 480-442-0228.

Professional Referral Readiness Assessment

Circle the statement which is most true for you

1. Do you have at least 2 years' experience in residential real estate?

   - Yes   10 points
   - No   0 points

2. Do you have a team of at least 4 real estate agents or the desire to build a successful team?

   - Yes   10 points
   - No   0 points

3. Do you enjoy presenting to groups of business professionals?

   - Yes   10 points
   - No   0 points

4. Are your presentation skills polished?

   - Yes   10 points
   - No   0 points

5. Do you instill a level of confidence in others?

   - Yes   10 points
   - No   0 points

6. Do you enjoy networking opportunities?

   - Yes   10 points
   - No   0 points

7. Do you have access to professional short sale negotiators?

   - Yes   10 points
   - No   0 points

8. Are you willing to work complex real estate transactions?

   - Yes   10 points
   - No   0 points

9. Do you have systems and processes in place to track and manage your transactions?

- Yes   10 points
- No   0 points

10. Do you enjoy working "outside the box"?

- Yes   10 points
- No   0 points

How did you do?

- 90+: Great job. You are a textbook candidate for working with The Professional Referral Solution. Call our office at (phone number?) to discuss opportunities.

- 70–89: Good job. You are likely a good candidate to working with professional referrals. We would like to speak with you to see if we are right fit for you.

- 60–69: There are some areas where you may need to improve before working with professional referrals. You can visit our website (website?) for more information.

- Below 60: you are probably not a good candidate for working with professional referrals. With experience that could change over time. If you find your score improves, please reach out to us for more information.

When complete email back to: **S4Info@gmail.com** and we'll be in touch with next steps.

Name: _____

Company Name: _____

Website: _____

Phone Number: _____

Email Address: _____

An Alternative Form of Lead Generation

This book is intended for real estate team leaders as well as agents who are in the process of growing a team.

Lead generation is not a one-size-fits-all approach. Cold calling and door knocking are proven methods but also result in high agent turnover, continuous recruiting, typically a low sales volume per team member, and face it … most agents hate it.

This book offers an alternative in the form of building a professional referral network. Why knock on 25 doors looking for a client when you could knock on one door and receive 25 referrals? Of course you need the right scripts, processes, systems, and tools to be effective.

In the book I discuss the advantages to building a professional referral network and how it helped me grow a $50-million+ per-year real estate business with just 9 people. Yes, my agents each close over $5.5 million on average and I have no turnover.

The book provides the basics. The next step is to determine if this system is a good fit for you and if you are a good fit for it.

Go to **www.s4grouprealestate.com/next-steps** and request more information.